ANIMALS AT RISK

MOUNTAIN GORILLAS AT RISK
SAVING THESE GREAT APES

BY KATHRYN CLAY

CAPSTONE PRESS
a capstone imprint

Published by Capstone Press, an imprint of Capstone
1710 Roe Crest Drive, North Mankato, Minnesota 56003
capstonepub.com

Copyright © 2025 by Capstone. All rights reserved. No part of this publication may be reproduced in whole or in part, or stored in a retrieval system, or transmitted in any form or by any means, electronic, mechanical, photocopying, recording, or otherwise, without written permission of the publisher.

Library of Congress Cataloging-in-Publication Data is available on the Library of Congress website

ISBN: 9798875221958 (hardcover)
ISBN: 9798875221903 (paperback)
ISBN: 9798875221910 (ebook PDF)

Summary: Mountain gorillas are strong, smart, and social, but they are at risk of extinction. Readers will learn what is putting these great apes in danger, including poaching, habitat loss, and disease, as well as what people are doing to help them.

Editorial Credits
Editor: Ashley Kuehl; Designer: Elyse White; Media Researcher: Jo Miller; Production Specialist: Tori Abraham

Image Credits
Alamy: Liam White, 19; Getty Images: Ibrahim Suha Derbent, 15, iStock/GlobalP, 24, iStock/GorazdBertalanic, cover, iStock/Oksana Ermak, 29 (twig pile), iStock/Ozbalci, 13, iStock/Rixipix, 14, iStock/zampe238, 18, Manuel ROMARIS, 11 (top), Mark Newman, 25, Musiime P Muramura/500px, 5, Paul Souders, 16, schleicher.hannes, 7; Shutterstock: Bhaskara Adrian, 17 (gorilla silhouette), Daniel Lamborn, 8, DeawSS, 4 (heart icon), imranhridoy, 4 (trees icon), Kiki Dohmeier, 12, Logoinspires_1, 17 (head silhouette), Mathias Sunke, 21, MERCURY studio, 27, nexusby, 4 (temperature icon), Ortis, 29 (leaves), PhotocechCZ, 28, SNeG17, 29 (paint), Stefan Balaz, 4 (arrow icon), Tony Stock, 29 (box), Vector Artworks (gorilla head icon), throughout, Viktor Tanasiichuk, 11 (map), xpixel, 29 (modeling clay); Superstock: Eric Remsberg/Visual & Written, 23

Design Elements
Shutterstock: Textures and backgrounds, Pixels Park

Any additional websites and resources referenced in this book are not maintained, authorized, or sponsored by Capstone. All product and company names are trademarks™ or registered® trademarks of their respective holders.

Printed and bound in China. 006276

TABLE OF CONTENTS

CHAPTER 1
A DAY IN THE LIFE 5

CHAPTER 2
GORILLAS UP CLOSE 10

CHAPTER 3
ENDANGERED 18

CHAPTER 4
HOW TO HELP 24

GLOSSARY	30
READ MORE	31
INTERNET SITES	31
INDEX	32
ABOUT THE AUTHOR	32

Words in **bold** are in the glossary.

WHAT MAKES AN ANIMAL ENDANGERED?

NUMBER OF ANIMALS:
VERY LOW OR SHRINKING FAST

HABITAT LOSS:
BIG DECREASE IN NATURAL HABITAT

RANGE REDUCTION:
SHRINKING AREA WHERE IT CAN LIVE

BREEDING DECLINE:
FEWER ANIMALS HAVING YOUNG

THREATS:
HIGH RISK OF POACHING, DISEASE, OR CLIMATE CHANGE

CHAPTER 1
A DAY IN THE LIFE

In a misty African forest, a mountain gorilla rises with the sun. It joins its family to search for leaves and fruit. After eating, the gorilla rests in the shade. It **grooms** and plays with the other gorillas.

The gorilla's family looks for food again in the afternoon. They might travel short distances, but the gorillas stay close to their home area. Soon evening approaches. The gorilla builds its own nest on the forest floor.

A gorilla sits in Uganda's Mgahinga Gorilla National Park.

SOCIAL LIFE

Mountain gorillas are strong, smart, and social. They spend most of their day eating and resting. They wake up early to look for food. Sometimes they eat small insects. But most of their diet is leaves, stems, and fruits. They use their strong teeth to chew tough plants.

Gorillas communicate through sounds and movements. They have many types of sounds, including grunts, roars, and screams. A gorilla might grunt to show happiness. It might roar to warn others of danger. Gorillas also use body language to communicate. They hug to show affection. Or they beat their chests to show power.

One young gorilla roars while playing with another young gorilla.

IN DANGER

Mountain gorillas are important to the forests where they live. Their big appetites help control plant growth. But these gentle giants face many dangers in the wild.

A gorilla feeds on plants in Bwindi Impenetrable Forest in Uganda.

Threats have made it hard for gorillas to survive. These include habitat loss, **poaching**, and disease. In the 1980s, gorillas were officially listed as **endangered**. **Conservation** groups have worked hard to save gorillas. Since 2010, the mountain gorilla population has more than doubled. Scientists counted about 480 gorillas in 2010. Now their numbers are over 1,000. But the animals are still at risk.

GORILLA TRIVIA

QUESTION: How does gorilla poop help the environment?

ANSWER: Gorillas spread seeds in their droppings. That helps plants grow in new places.

CHAPTER 2
GORILLAS UP CLOSE

Africa is a huge continent. But mountain gorillas only live in three countries. They make their homes high in the mountains of Rwanda, Uganda, and the Democratic Republic of Congo (DRC). These places have cooler temperatures than many parts of Africa. Long, thick fur keeps the gorillas warm. Their fur and tough skin also protect them from bites and scratches.

Gorillas bend branches and leaves to create a soft place to sleep. Each night they build a new nest on the ground or in trees. Sometimes, their new nest is right next to their old nest.

EASTERN SPECIES

Mountain gorillas are part of the eastern gorilla **species**. So are eastern lowland gorillas. They live in tropical rainforests with warmer temperatures. Eastern lowland gorillas are bigger than mountain gorillas. Both kinds are at risk of dying out.

Gorillas live in groups called troops. Each troop has between two and 40 gorillas. Most troops have 10 to 20 members. Each group is led by an older male called a silverback. As males get older, they grow silver hair on their backs. That's where the name comes from.

A silverback walks through the grass in Rwanda.

Mountain gorillas climb trees to gather fruit.

The silverback is very protective, especially of young ones. If a **predator** threatens the group, the silverback will fight to protect his family. Females also protect their infants. They carry the babies on their backs or bellies. The babies' hands and feet hang on tightly. Mothers groom the babies to keep them clean.

GORILLA TRIVIA

QUESTION: How long do gorillas sleep?

ANSWER: Gorillas sleep about 12 hours each night.

LIFE CYCLE

Gorillas have a life cycle similar to humans. Female gorillas usually have one baby at a time. Baby gorillas weigh about 4 to 5 pounds (1.8 to 2.2 kilograms) at birth. They depend on their mothers for food and protection. They share her nest.

A baby gorilla grips its mother's fur to hang on.

Baby gorillas play with their mothers and with other young gorillas.

Gorillas become more independent around age three. They start to explore but stay close to their troop. Young gorillas play a lot. They wrestle and climb trees. This helps them build strength and skills.

About half of young male gorillas stay with their troop. Others leave to form their own troops. That happens around ages 11 to 15.

GORILLA TRIVIA

QUESTION: How long do mountain gorillas live?

ANSWER: They can live for 35 to 40 years in the wild.

15

GENTLE BUT STRONG

Despite their size and strength, gorillas tend to be gentle. They prefer to avoid conflicts. They only become fierce if they feel threatened. They may fight if their troop is in danger. When a silverback senses danger, he beats his chest. The loud drumming sound travels far. The action shows his strength and warns others to stay away. If predators come too close, gorillas defend themselves. Their sharp teeth give powerful bites.

Gorillas have sharp teeth and strong bodies.

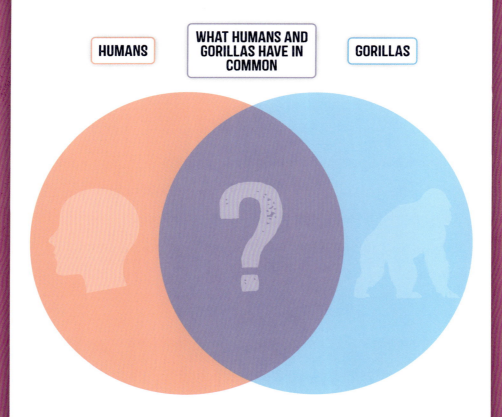

ALIKE AND DIFFERENT

Gorillas and humans are closely related. In fact, we share 98 percent of our **DNA**. We have a lot in common. But there are also some major differences. Use the information from this book and your own research to explore how we're alike and different. Ideas include how we look, how we live, and how we behave. Then make a Venn diagram, as seen above. This tool helps you compare and contrast.

CHAPTER 3
ENDANGERED

When a species is endangered, it means that very few of the animals are left. Just over 1,000 mountain gorillas are left in the wild. Each one is precious. Without conservation efforts, gorillas could become **extinct**.

DIAN FOSSEY

Dian Fossey studied mountain gorillas in Africa. She lived in the mountains of Rwanda to learn how gorillas live and behave. Fossey grew close to the gorillas. She gave them names. She watched how they interacted with one another. These observations helped her better understand their social groups and family life.

Fossey also worked hard to protect gorillas from poachers. She taught others about conservation. She set up patrols to stop poachers. Her work helped to save mountain gorillas from extinction.

ENVIRONMENTAL RISKS

One of the biggest dangers to mountain gorillas is habitat loss. Forests are being cut down to make room for farms, roads, and buildings. Gorillas have less space to live, find food, and raise their young.

Mountain gorillas are also at risk of getting sick. They are closely related to humans. They can catch many of the same illnesses. Disease can spread quickly through a gorilla troop. Gorillas don't have the same immune system as humans. That means these illnesses can be deadly. Even a simple cold can be dangerous for a gorilla.

Many trees have been cut down in the mountains of Bwindi Forest in Uganda.

HUMAN-MADE RISKS

Another major threat to mountain gorillas is poaching. It is illegal to hunt or capture mountain gorillas. But poaching still happens. Some people hunt gorillas for their meat and fur. Others sell their body parts as trophies or for medicines. Baby gorillas are sometimes captured to be sold as pets. Adults may be killed trying to protect them.

Poaching hurts the small population of mountain gorillas that are left. Some groups have set up safe areas for gorillas. Park rangers patrol these areas to keep poachers away.

A park ranger walks through Virunga National Park in the DRC.

GORILLA TRIVIA

QUESTION: How big do gorillas get?

ANSWER: Adult gorillas can weigh up to 440 pounds (200 kg). They are about as tall as adult humans.

23

CHAPTER 4
HOW TO HELP

Many people are working to help and protect mountain gorillas. Some people pass laws to protect gorillas from poachers. Others raise awareness in local communities.

A gorilla family in Virunga National Park in the DRC.

GROUPS WORKING TO HELP MOUNTAIN GORILLAS

African Wildlife Foundation: Buys and donates land for gorillas to live safely.

The Gorilla Organization: Supports and protects local people and the environment; patrols gorilla habitat to stop poaching.

International Gorilla Conservation Programme: Conducts research and education on mountain gorillas.

World Wildlife Foundation: Protects gorilla habitats and stops hunting in protected areas among local communities.

KIDS CAN HELP TOO

Mountain gorillas may live far away from you, but people everywhere can do things to help protect them. One way to help is to raise awareness about mountain gorillas. Kids can share information with friends and family. A school project on gorillas can teach others about them. The more people know about gorillas, the more they will support efforts to protect them.

People can also make responsible choices. They can avoid products that cause habitat destruction. For example, **harvesting** palm oil often involves cutting down forests where gorillas live. Families can buy palm oil from **sustainable** companies. Or they can choose not to buy it.

Palm oil is used in cooking. It comes from palm fruits.

Mountain gorillas teach us about the importance of family, community, and caring for our planet. By protecting them and their habitats, we also protect the world we share with all creatures.

GORILLA HABITAT

Make a mountain gorilla habitat. You'll need a cardboard box, art supplies, twigs, and leaves. Paint the inside of the box. Include the sky, mountains, and forests. Glue down pebbles and dirt for a forest floor. Use twigs and leaves to build a gorilla bed. Crumple tissue paper to create bushy plants. Mold a silverback out of modeling clay. Then share your creation with friends and family. Remind them to help save gorillas.

GLOSSARY

conservation (khan-sur-VAY-shun)—wise use and protection of natural resources

DNA (DEE-ehn-ay)—the part of the body that carries genetic material passed down from parents to children

endangered (en-DANE-jurd)—at risk of dying out

extinct (ik-STINGKT)—when all the members of a species are no longer living; an extinct animal species has died out

groom (GRUME)—to clean and comb fur or hair

harvest (HAHR-vist)—to gather crops that are ripe

poaching (POHCH-eeng)—illegal hunting or fishing

predator (PRED-uh-tur)—an animal that hunts other animals for food

species (SPEE-sheez)—a group of plants or animals that share common characteristics

sustainable (suh-STAY-nuh-buhl)—made in a way that causes little or no damage to the environment

READ MORE

Clasky, Leonard. *The Mountain Gorilla*. New York: Gareth Stevens Publishing, 2023.

Gish, Melissa. *Gorillas*. Mankato, MN: Creative Education, 2024.

Grady, Tyler. *Gorilla: Fascinating Animal Facts for Kids*. Osprey, FL: Dylanna Press, 2024.

INTERNET SITES

The Gorilla Foundation
koko.org

Mountain Gorilla
kids.nationalgeographic.com/animals/mammals/facts/mountain-gorilla

Mountain Gorilla
worldwildlife.org/species/mountain-gorilla

INDEX

communication, 6, 7, 16
conservation, 9, 18, 19, 22, 24, 25, 26
diseases, 4, 9, 20
eastern lowland gorillas, 11
food, 5, 6, 8, 13, 14, 20
Fossey, Dian, 19
fur, 10, 14, 22
habitats, 4, 8, 9, 10, 11, 20, 25, 26, 28, 29
life cycle, 14
life span, 15

nests, 5, 10, 14
poaching, 4, 9, 19, 22, 24, 25
predators, 13, 16
silverbacks, 12, 13, 16, 29
size, 16, 23
sleeping, 10, 13
teeth, 6, 16
troops, 12, 15, 16, 20
young, 4, 7, 13, 14, 15, 20, 22

ABOUT THE AUTHOR

Kathryn Clay has written more than 100 nonfiction books for kids. Her books cover a wide range of topics, including everything from sign language to space travel. When she's not writing, Kathryn works at a college, helping students develop their critical thinking and study skills. She holds master's degrees in literature and creative writing from Minnesota State University, Mankato.

Kathryn lives in southern Minnesota with her family and an energetic goldendoodle. Together, they make sustainable, eco-friendly choices whenever possible.